The World's Biggest Piss Offs

SIDNEY S. PRASAD

ISBN:1927676320
ISBN-13: 978-1-927676-32-5

DEDICATION

I dedicate this book to my good friend Navin. Bro, I truly believe our friendship is the eighth wonder of the world. After two decades of pulling pranks on each other, mildly screwing each other over, and trading home cities, it's amazing that we are still close like brothers and can look back and reflect on the good times!

CONTENTS

ACKNOWLEDGMENTS

My heart goes out to anyone who has ever been annoyed by another person's sheer ignorance. It only gets worse when the person who is making your life hell is within arm's reach of you, ranging from pesky neighbors to irritating roommates. Anytime one dines at a restaurant or goes somewhere in public, they're at risk of rubbing elbows with someone who can turn their life upside down. I understand society's frustrations, as I too have had my share of sharing cabs with smelly people and witnessing my neighbor's dog stealing food off my barbecue.

Each of us has a personal threshold for frustration, and I wrote this book to poke at *The World's Biggest Piss Offs*!

1 PISS OFF!

Doesn't it piss you off when your boss gives you a wake-up call?

Doesn't it piss you off when you wake up in a bathtub full of ice and you're missing some organs?

Doesn't it piss you off when you find an eviction notice on your front door?

Doesn't it piss you off when you walk into a convenience store and interrupt a burglary?

Doesn't it piss you off when you're attempting to call in sick and your company's phone lines are down?

Doesn't it piss you off when your welfare check bounces?

Doesn't it piss you off when you discover a naked picture of yourself on the cover of a magazine?

Doesn't it piss you off when you wake up in a casket?

Doesn't it piss you off when a kid you've never seen before calls you Daddy?

Doesn't it piss you off when you have to use your Visa to pay your MasterCard?

Doesn't it piss you off when your blind date ends up being your ex-spouse?

Doesn't it piss you off when your wife says, "Good morning, Paul" when your name is Bob?

Doesn't it piss you off when you call 911 and you get put on hold?

Doesn't it piss you off when your bankcard declines for a $2 purchase?

Doesn't it piss you off when you wake up in a hospital room with your friends watching you drool?

Doesn't it piss you off when the girl you picked up at the bar ends up being a guy?

Doesn't it piss you off when your boss tells you not to bother taking off your coat?

Doesn't it piss you off when you kiss someone with braces and both of your braces get stuck together?

Doesn't it piss you off when your twin brother forgets your birthday?

Doesn't it piss you off when you wake up in a drunk tank?

Doesn't it piss you off when you catch your girlfriend in your roommate's pajamas?

Doesn't it piss you off when you drop burning hot coffee on your crotch?

Doesn't it piss you off when you know the Grim Reaper is waiting for you?

Doesn't it piss you off when you are lying on the ground with chalk drawn around your body?

Doesn't it piss you off when a homeless person offers you money?

Doesn't it piss you off when your blind date points out the toilet paper stuck to your shoe?

Doesn't it piss you off when you step in dog shit five minutes before a job interview?

Doesn't it piss you off when you accidently show up to work on a statutory holiday?

Doesn't it piss you off when you catch your stockbroker hitchhiking out of town?

Doesn't it piss you off when you stick two contact lenses in the same eye?

Doesn't it piss you off when you find hookers picketing on your driveway?

Doesn't it piss you off when you get delivered a half-eaten pizza?

Doesn't it piss you off when you fall into a coma?

Doesn't it piss you off when you wake up in a body bag?

Doesn't it piss you off when you see your boyfriend's picture on a "Wanted" poster?

Doesn't it piss you off when you find a bankruptcy lock on your employer's door?

Doesn't it piss you off when you accidently hit a cop car?

Doesn't it piss you off when you get your peepee stuck in your zipper?

Doesn't it piss you off when you wake up in jail with a condom up your ass?

Doesn't it piss you off when your doctor calls you in to discuss your venereal disease test results?

Doesn't it piss you off when your cat poops in your cereal?

Doesn't it piss you off when your mother-in-law shows up for a surprise visit?

Doesn't it piss you off when the person sitting next to you on an eight-hour airline flight hasn't showered in ten years?

Doesn't it piss you off when your windshield is covered in bird shit?

Doesn't it piss you off you when you discover the woman sleeping next to you is married?

Doesn't it piss you off when someone steals the prize out of your cereal box?

Doesn't it piss you off when your neighbor decides to cut their lawn at six in the morning?

Doesn't it piss you off when you wake up in Las Vegas with a wedding band on your finger?

Doesn't it piss you off when you forget to close the window and your bird escapes?

Doesn't it piss you off when your car transmission blows up and your warranty expired yesterday?

Doesn't it piss you off when you forget that you had a final exam scheduled today?

Doesn't it piss you off when a collector gives you a rude awakening?

Doesn't it piss you off when the library refuses to lend you a book?

Doesn't it piss you off when your fiancée dumps you via telegram?

Doesn't it piss you off when you get tipped in Monopoly money?

Doesn't it piss you off when a hooker doesn't want your company?

Doesn't it piss you off when some asshole tells you that it's the first day of the rest of your life?

Doesn't it piss you off when you run out of gas on the way to the bank machine?

Doesn't it piss you off when you fail a survey?

Doesn't it piss you off when you trip over a cordless phone?

Doesn't it piss you off when you have to put a Big Mac on layaway?

Doesn't it piss you off when you pickpocket someone with two dollars in their wallet?

Doesn't it piss you off when your waiter offers you a senior's discount and you are only 30 years old?

Doesn't it piss you off when your fortune cookie is missing the message?

Doesn't it piss you off when your date forgets to flush the toilet and leaves you a present?

Doesn't it piss you off when the DEA has a search warrant for your roommate's room?

Doesn't it piss you off when you get fired while you are on vacation?

Doesn't it piss you off when you give someone the finger and they end up being your new boss?

Doesn't it piss you off when you wake up with an animal on top of you, and you don't own any pets?

Doesn't it piss you off when you don't recognize the person sleeping next to you, and you're late for your wedding?

Doesn't it piss you off when you wake up in a dumpster?

Doesn't it piss you off when a hostess refuses to let you in without a reservation?

Doesn't it piss you off when it takes two hours to watch *60 Minutes*?

Doesn't it piss you off when a jury finds you guilty of a crime you didn't commit?

Doesn't it piss you off when you lose the winning ticket for the state lottery?

Doesn't it piss you off when a telemarketer voluntarily takes you off their list?

Doesn't it piss you off when a nudist camp park ranger asks you to put your clothes back on?

Doesn't it piss you off when you're the first one chosen to be a hostage in a bank robbery?

Doesn't it piss you off when you lock your car keys in the getaway car?

Doesn't it piss you off when your date forgets their wallet?

Doesn't it piss you off when run out of toilet paper and have major diarrhea?

Doesn't it piss you off when you call 911 and a mute answers the phone?

Doesn't it piss you off when you get confused for a secondhand-store flyer model?

Doesn't it piss you off when you discover that you used an expired condom last night?

Doesn't it piss you off when your brother tells you "yo' mama" jokes?

Doesn't it piss you off when a burglar breaks into your house and doesn't find anything worth stealing?

Doesn't it piss you off when you remove your clothes and your date laughs at you?

Doesn't it piss you off when you have to use three credit cards to pay for a bagel?

Doesn't it piss you off when you get fired from the mental hospital for depressing all the patients?

Doesn't it piss you off when you're an undercover cop posing as a hooker and none of the Johns want to pick you up?

Doesn't it piss you off when you get fired from a volunteer assignment?

Doesn't it piss you off when people recognize you from your last life?

Doesn't it piss you off when the sandwich artist making your lunch quits before completing your sandwich?

Doesn't it piss you off when you get a sex change and people tell you to get another one?

Doesn't it piss you off when you have to take out a second mortgage to pay for a pizza?

Doesn't it piss you off when nobody shows up to your surprise birthday party?

Doesn't it piss you off when the health inspector evacuates the restaurant where you're having dinner?

2 ANNOYING PEOPLE

Doesn't it piss you off when someone claims to have an emergency and needs your cell phone, and once they get your phone, they order a pizza?

Doesn't it piss you off when someone questions a garage-sale host on their return policy?

Doesn't it piss you off when someone writes "NAME" on their name tag?

Doesn't it piss you off when someone walks around with a visible wedgie?

Doesn't it piss you off when someone makes sexual moaning sounds each time someone is about to hit the ball on a golf course?

Doesn't it piss you off when someone passes behind you at the casino and yells out, "Cheater?"

Doesn't it piss you off when someone asks the mall Santa Claus if he is legally allowed to work around kids?

Doesn't it piss you off when someone pushes a CPR dummy off a tall building?

Doesn't it piss you off when someone parks behind a cop car and accuses the cop of speeding?

Doesn't it piss you off when someone picks their nose with the bank teller's pen?

Doesn't it piss you off when someone takes fifty things to a twelve-items-or-less express cashier?

Doesn't it piss you off when someone goes to the grocery store, takes a bite out of an apple, and sticks it back in the bin?

Doesn't it piss you off when someone closes your laptop computer for you?

Doesn't it piss you off when someone sneezes and wipes their nose on their sleeve?

Doesn't it piss you off when someone calls the Operator and asks for the phone number for the Operator?

Doesn't it piss you off when someone keeps saying "man" to a woman with short hair?

Doesn't it piss you off when someone questions the receptionist on how many years of medical experience the doctor has?

Doesn't it piss you off when someone asks an obese male when his baby is due?

Doesn't it piss you off when someone addresses their waitress by the name "Flo?"

Doesn't it piss you off when someone sitting at an auction continuously yells out "Bingo!" each time the auctioneer speaks?

Doesn't it piss you off when someone phones up random salespeople and says, "I'm not interested?"

Doesn't it piss you off when someone throws their garbage in other people's trash cans?

Doesn't it piss you off when someone sits next to you on the bus, writes down questions on a notepad, and passes it back and forth to you—and then, when they arrive at their stop, says "thank you" and walks away?

Doesn't it piss you off when someone attends a funeral and keeps winking at the priest while he is giving his sermon?

Doesn't it piss you off when someone avoids eye contact while talking?

Doesn't it piss you off when someone pigs out at a buffet, then goes to an amusement park and rides the roller coaster all day long?

Doesn't it piss you off when someone steps in dog shit before lining up at the Department of Motor Vehicles?

Doesn't it piss you off when someone asks the sandwich artist making their lunch if they washed their hands?

Doesn't it piss you off when someone walks around town with toilet paper hanging out of their pants?

Doesn't it piss you off when someone continuously asks the other patrons in the restaurant for menu recommendations?

Doesn't it piss you off when someone doesn't take a shower for a month and goes to the movie theater on opening night?

Doesn't it piss you off when someone chews with their mouth open?

Doesn't it piss you off when you're making out with someone in a car and the person parked next to you purposely sets their car alarm off and walks into the mall?

Doesn't it piss you off when someone clips their toenails in the back of a taxicab?

Doesn't it piss you off when someone drives by a cop while talking into a toy cell phone?

Doesn't it piss you off when you're in a traffic jam and someone goes outside and takes a leak?

Doesn't it piss you off when the person in front of you at the counter keeps entering the wrong bankcard PIN after a couple of tries?

Doesn't it piss you off when someone takes a raunchy shit in the hardware store showroom toilet?

Doesn't it piss you off when someone who weighs over 400 pounds walks around town wearing Spandex?

Doesn't it piss you off when senior citizens make out in public?

Doesn't it piss you off when someone strips down to their underwear while washing their clothes at the laundromat?

Doesn't it piss you off when someone who doesn't know you keeps waving to you?

Doesn't it piss you off when someone puts their Christmas lights up in July?

Doesn't it piss you off when someone asks a panhandler if they can break a hundred dollar bill?

Doesn't it piss you off when someone breastfeeds a toy doll on the subway?

Doesn't it piss you off when someone knocks on the toilet stall wall and asks if you have loose change?

Doesn't it piss you off when someone goes to City Hall and pays their property taxes in pennies?

Doesn't it piss you off when someone makes a scene at the library and pretends that they are locked inside?

Doesn't it piss you off when someone coughs on the payphone receiver before passing it to you?

Doesn't it piss you off when someone ugly personalizes their business card with their picture?

Doesn't it piss you off when someone leaves their cell phone ringer on high volume at the library?

Doesn't it piss you off when someone walks around the shopping mall with an open umbrella?

Doesn't it piss you off when someone rides the escalator in the opposite direction?

Doesn't it piss you off when some stranger knocks on your door and asks if they can use your shitter?

Doesn't it piss you off when someone phones a daycare and leaves a message for the kids to act their age?

Doesn't it piss you off when someone lights up a cigarette in the nonsmoking section of a restaurant?

Doesn't it piss you off when someone whispers their order in a fast food drive-thru?

Doesn't it piss you off when someone dresses up like a gladiator and chases you with a plastic sword?

Doesn't it piss you off when someone points and laughs at random people?

Doesn't it piss you off when someone changes their barber's radio station without his permission?

Doesn't it piss you off when you're sitting at a check stop and the person in front of you tells the cop that they drank a keg?

Doesn't it piss you off when someone repeats every question the sandwich artist asks at the submarine shop?

Doesn't it piss you off when someone starts doing the Running Man while a country song is playing?

Doesn't it piss you off when someone gets into a vulgar argument with themselves in a crowded elevator?

Doesn't it piss you off when someone sprays their crotch with the tester cologne and winks at the salesperson?

Doesn't it piss you off when someone goes to a buffet and hides all the toilet paper in the washroom ceiling?

Doesn't it piss you off when someone blows bubbles in an elevator?

Doesn't it piss you off when someone pays for a bag of chips using three different credit cards?

Doesn't it piss you off when someone uses a gas station washroom and leaves the key inside?

Doesn't it piss you off when someone wearing a bib and with a fork and knife in their shirt pocket goes buck wild in the bulk food section of the supermarket?

Doesn't it piss you off when someone parks behind a parked car and honks their horn for a half hour?

Doesn't it piss you off when someone heckles a news reporter until they swear on camera?

Doesn't it piss you off when someone wears a glow-in-the-dark outfit in the nightclub?

Doesn't it piss you off when some pervert brings a pair of binoculars to the nude beach and stares at everyone?

Doesn't it piss you off someone yells out, "Driver, close the door—and step on it, boy!" as you're running for the bus?

Doesn't it piss you off when someone phones an Italian restaurant and asks if they know where they can score some good pasta?

Doesn't it piss you off when someone asks you to turn down the volume on your crying baby?

Doesn't it piss you off when someone reads a dirty magazine upside-down while listening to a pastor deliver his sermon?

Doesn't it piss you off when someone brings their grandparents to the nude beach?

Doesn't it piss you off when someone stands facing everybody in the elevator?

Doesn't it piss you off when someone asks a shoe shiner if he will suck on their big toe for an extra dollar?

Doesn't it piss you off when someone puts on a porn DVD in the department store's home entertainment section?

Doesn't it piss you off when someone videotapes random people eating their dinners on restaurant patios?

Doesn't it piss you off when the person sitting behind you places a piece of hair on their plate as they run to the washroom?

Doesn't it piss you off when someone who can talk normally purposely stutters their order in the fast food drive-thru?

Doesn't it piss you off when someone calls up a funeral parlor and ask them if they're open for the graveyard shift?

Doesn't it piss you off when someone takes a taxicab to another taxicab?

Doesn't it piss you off when someone in the next toilet stall continuously asks you questions while you're taking a dump?

3 IRRITATING

Doesn't it piss you off when you're napping at the airport and someone wakes you up to ask you for the time?

Doesn't it piss you off when someone scratches their crotch before taking a free sample at the supermarket?

Doesn't it piss you off when someone returns something they bought at your garage sale?

Doesn't it piss you off when someone uses their fingers as quotation marks each time they speak?

Doesn't it piss you off when someone eats their cereal with chopsticks?

Doesn't it piss you off when someone asks a priest if they're religious?

Doesn't it piss you off when someone forgets to flush the toilet after eating corn?

Doesn't it piss you off when someone wipes their crappy ass with a towel and hangs the towel back up?

Doesn't it piss you off when someone approaches a senior citizen and asks them to produce some proof of age?

Doesn't it piss you off when someone barges in front of the line at McDonald's and states that they have reservations?

Doesn't it piss you off when some random stranger follows you around the shopping mall for a couple of hours?

Doesn't it piss you off when someone completely nude asks you for directions?

Doesn't it piss you off when someone watches porn on the library computer?

Doesn't it piss you off when someone takes a crap and throws the used toilet paper in the garbage?

Doesn't it piss you off when someone names their dog, "Dog?"

Doesn't it piss you off when someone blatantly accuses the mall Santa Claus of being a fraud?

Doesn't it piss you off when someone cuts their lawn with scissors?

Doesn't it piss you off when someone asks a panhandler if they can break a traveler's check?

Doesn't it piss you off when someone interrupts a kissing session to ask you for the phone number of the police?

Doesn't it piss you off when someone lets out the loudest farts during the silent and suspenseful moments of a movie?

Doesn't it piss you off when you're taking a dump in a public washroom and someone turns off the lights?

Doesn't it piss you off when someone pretends to drink a breathalyzer like a beer?

Doesn't it piss you off when your friend borrows a shitload of money from you and then changes their phone number?

Doesn't it piss you off when someone goes jogging with a ski mask on and constantly takes quick glances behind them?

Doesn't it piss you off when someone asks you who you voted for at the polling place?

Doesn't it piss you off when someone pretends to work at a store and gives bogus advice on products and services?

Doesn't it piss you off when someone has a garage sale in the middle of winter?

Doesn't it piss you off when someone pees on your toilet?

Doesn't it piss you off when someone plays with a yo-yo in the bank line?

Doesn't it piss you off when someone goes to a steakhouse and asks for the vegetarian menu?

Doesn't it piss you off when someone drinks coffee with handcuffs on?

Doesn't it piss you off when someone gives you a maxed-out gift card for Christmas?

Doesn't it piss you off when someone brings a universal remote control to the department store and sabotages the salespeople's TV presentations?

Doesn't it piss you off when someone sneezes on the buttons of the vending machine?

Doesn't it piss you off when someone takes a bath in the wishing well at the shopping center?

Doesn't it piss you off when someone says the word "like" before each word?

Doesn't it piss you off when someone yells, "Shut the fuck up" to the screaming vendors at the ball game?

Doesn't it piss you off when someone hogs the payphone and files their nails as they're talking?

Doesn't it piss you off when someone goes to a nudist camp and flashes people with their clothes on?

Doesn't it piss you off when someone yells "Owwww" as soon as they sit beside you?

Doesn't it piss you off when your girlfriend asks you where the sexually transmitted disease clinic is located?

Doesn't it piss you off when someone asks a striking picketer where the job applications are?

Doesn't it piss you off when someone asks a hooker what her refund policy is?

Doesn't it piss you off when someone has a picnic in the mall food court?

Doesn't it piss you off when someone tries to order a Big Mac at a coffee shop?

Doesn't it piss you off when someone R.S.V.P.s to an event with, "I'll think about it?"

Doesn't it piss you off when the guy pissing next to you puts out his hand and introduces himself?

Doesn't it piss you off when someone skips rope in a graveyard?

Doesn't it piss you off when someone records random people's conversations on the subway and plays them back to them?

Doesn't it piss you off when someone leaves a baby doll on your doorstep with a message saying "I know what you did last summer!" attached?

Doesn't it piss you off when a window cleaner keeps giving you the middle finger?

Doesn't it piss you off when an adult sticks their tongue out at a two-year-old in a passing vehicle?

Doesn't it piss you off when someone attempts to return used, soiled, inside-out underwear?

Doesn't it piss you off when some customer answers a ringing phone at a department store?

Doesn't it piss you off when someone asks an obese man if his breasts are real?

Doesn't it piss you off when someone drags their feet when they are walking?

Doesn't it piss you off when someone asks a pregnant woman if she is a virgin?

Doesn't it piss you off when someone files a police report claim pertaining to Goldilocks stealing their porridge?

Doesn't it piss you off when someone makes a speech in sign language?

Doesn't it piss you off when someone ignores the restaurant hostess and seats themselves?

Doesn't it piss you off when someone at the grocery store licks the cream off cookies and sticks them back in the bag?

Doesn't it piss you off when someone asks a government worker to explain their job description in detail?

Doesn't it piss you off when someone asks an old lady if she is going to the Golden Girls reunion?

Doesn't it piss you off when someone purposely shits their pants at the beginning of an eight-hour flight?

Doesn't it piss you off when someone asks a pilot if they like to get high?

Doesn't it piss you off when you're the only one in the movie theatre and some idiot comes and sits right next to you?

Doesn't it piss you off when someone changes their kid's poopy diapers on the cafeteria counter?

Doesn't it piss you off when the person sitting next to you on an airplane falls asleep drooling on you?

Doesn't it piss you off when someone removes their smelly socks during rush hour on the subway?

Doesn't it piss you off when someone asks three people within earshot of each other the exact same question?

Doesn't it piss you off when someone who forgot to wear underwear walks around all day with their zipper down?

Doesn't it piss you off when someone hits on the people coming into the emergency room at the hospital?

Doesn't it piss you off when someone tells the security guard at the racetrack that the animals are horsing around?

Doesn't it piss you off when someone phones up the Madison, Wisconsin city hall and asks if they've got milk?

Doesn't it piss you off when someone offers his or her deodorant stick to everyone sitting in your row at the movie theatre?

Doesn't it piss you off when someone walks into your place, doesn't say "Hi," and opens your fridge?

Doesn't it piss you off when someone asks a person with a British accent what part of Australia they are from?

Doesn't it piss you off when someone asks a person with an Australian accent what part of Britain they are from?

Doesn't it piss you off when someone pours ketchup all over a CPR dummy and leaves it in an abandoned shopping cart?

Doesn't it piss you off when someone purposely says "word" after every second word?

Doesn't it piss you off when someone hands out an after-hours party flyer to a nonexistent location?

Doesn't it piss you off when someone invites all their friends to their house for a party and doesn't answer the door?

Doesn't it piss you off when someone mails out black envelopes with a message inside saying, "You just got blackmailed?"

Doesn't it piss you off when someone wears a beer shirt to rehab?

Doesn't it piss you off when someone walks around with sunglasses on during the night?

Doesn't it piss you off when someone farts on you as you are bench-pressing some heavy weights?

Doesn't it piss you off when someone flicks their headlights on and off at the drive-in movie theatre?

Doesn't it piss you off when someone eats fast food while on the treadmill at the gym?

Doesn't it piss you off when someone cranks the volume of their radio at a fishing hole?

Doesn't it piss you off when you're anorexic and someone mutters "You look fat" when you are trying on expensive clothes at Walmart?

Doesn't it piss you off when someone drops a bag of marbles in a crowded washroom?

Doesn't it piss you off when someone steals food from your plate and pretends to be invisible when you confront them?

Doesn't it piss you off when someone blows out your birthday candles for you?

Doesn't it piss you off when someone stands at the entrance of a movie theater and tells you how the movie is going to end?

Doesn't it piss you off when someone stares at a blank piece of paper for two hours?

Doesn't it piss you off when someone leaves the toilet seat up at a feminist rally?

Doesn't it piss you off when someone stands outside a restaurant window and picks their nose as they watch you eat?

4 RESTAURANTS

Doesn't it piss you off when someone pulls out a TV dinner from their purse and asks their waiter to heat it in the microwave?

Doesn't it piss you off when someone customizes the hell out of their meal by changing the sauce flavors, grilling instead of baking, and alternating the pasta shells?

Doesn't it piss you off when someone orders a Coke, and when it arrives, they tell their waiter that they wanted a Pepsi?

Doesn't it piss you off when someone asks their waiter if they have a LinkedIn profile?

Doesn't it piss you off when someone claps their hands every time their waiter brings them something?

Doesn't it piss you off when someone winks at a waiter as they erotically lick their fingers?

Doesn't it piss you off when a restaurant patron leaves condoms in between the sugar packets?

Doesn't it piss you off when someone raises their hand whenever they're attempting to get their waiter's attention?

Doesn't it piss you off when someone brings a jerrican to a restaurant that advertises "free refills" and demands that their waiter fill it up with pop?

Doesn't it piss you off when someone constantly drops their utensils and asks their waiter for replacements?

Doesn't it piss you off when someone asks their waiter if all the items on the menu are his best price?

Doesn't it piss you off when someone demands that their waiter honor their competitor's expired coupons?

Doesn't it piss you off when someone constantly requests items not listed on the menu?

Doesn't it piss you off when someone changes their baby at the table and gives the poopy diapers to their waiter?

Doesn't it piss you off when someone says, "Oh, shit. I pissed on myself again," as they walk out of the washroom, shaking their wet hands?

Doesn't it piss you off when someone brings outside beverages into the restaurant?

Doesn't it piss you off when someone clears their throat every time their waiter talks?

Doesn't it piss you off when someone dumps the entire contents of the complimentary mint jar into their purse?

Doesn't it piss you off when someone gives their waiter their car keys and asks him to park their vehicle?

Doesn't it piss you off when someone says the word "fucking" before each menu item that they're ordering?

Doesn't it piss you off when someone phones their waiter from their table requesting some extra napkins?

Doesn't it piss you off when someone brings their own coasters to the restaurant?

Doesn't it piss you off when someone plays with a remote control car while waiting for their food?

Doesn't it piss you off when someone questions the waiter about the restaurant's refund policy halfway through their meal?

Doesn't it piss you off when someone continually asks their waiter if they're getting charged for the free pop refills?

Doesn't it piss you off when someone tells their waiter that they refuse to sit at the table next to the shitter?

Doesn't it piss you off when someone takes their menu to the washroom?

Doesn't it piss you off when someone wears earmuffs the whole time they're in the restaurant…during mid-summer?

Doesn't it piss you off when someone traces their hand giving the middle finger on a napkin and leaves it with the check?

Doesn't it piss you off when someone wraps the tablecloth around their neck and uses it as a bib?

Doesn't it piss you off when someone uses binoculars to stare at other patrons' meals and tells their waiter they want that exact same meal?

Doesn't it piss you off when someone finishes their meal and asks their waiter for a discount?

Doesn't it piss you off when someone ignores their waiter each time he is talking and then complains to their dinner companion that they keep hearing voices?

Doesn't it piss you off when someone glues a quarter to their table as a tip?

Doesn't it piss you off when someone flosses their teeth while waiting for their food?

Doesn't it piss you off when someone asks their waiter if he is wearing deodorant?

Doesn't it piss you off when someone goes to a buffet and asks their waiter what the specials are?

Doesn't it piss you off when someone says "Shush" each time their waiter asks them a question?

Doesn't it piss you off when someone lets out the loudest fart and then gives their waiter a dirty look?

Doesn't it piss you off when someone sniffs the other patrons' food on their waiter's tray?

Doesn't it piss you off when someone solicits Avon and Tupperware products to other restaurant customers while waiting for their food?

Doesn't it piss you off when someone handcuffs one of their arms to their chair while eating lunch?

Doesn't it piss you off when someone takes a bite out of their food after their waiter agrees to take their meal back to the kitchen?

Doesn't it piss you off when someone discloses that they're in a rush and they need their waiter to produce their entire dinner within five minutes?

Doesn't it piss you off when someone keeps staring at their watch each time their waiter passes by while waiting for their meal?

Doesn't it piss you off when someone makes farting sounds every time their waiter passes by?

Doesn't it piss you off when someone makes loud moaning sounds after each bite?

Doesn't it piss you off when someone asks their waiter for nutritional information on every item on the menu?

Doesn't it piss you off when someone writes their order on a napkin and passes it to their waiter?

Doesn't it piss you off when someone continuously asks different waiters to bring them condiments and napkins?

Doesn't it piss you off when someone loosens their table legs before they leave the restaurant?

Doesn't it piss you off when someone stays an extra half hour after the restaurant's closing time?

Doesn't it piss you off when someone purposely drops ketchup on their lap and asks their waiter to clean it up?

Doesn't it piss you off when someone pays for their entire meal with unrolled pennies?

Doesn't it piss you off when someone leaves a picture of a naked senior citizen as a tip?

Doesn't it piss you off when someone asks their waiter if they're doing community service working at the restaurant?

Doesn't it piss you off when someone asks their waiter what do they want to do when they grow up?

Doesn't it piss you off when someone confuses the hell out of their waiter and orders in sign language?

Doesn't it piss you off when someone pays for their meal with four different credit cards?

Doesn't it piss you off when another restaurant patron borrows food off your plate?

Doesn't it piss you off when someone purposely takes four hours eating their meal when they notice a line forming outside the restaurant?

Doesn't it piss you off when someone asks their waiter if they can place their meal on a layaway plan?

Doesn't it piss you off when someone demands that their waiter wash his hands in front of them?

Doesn't it piss you off when someone screams out, "Hey, your zipper is undone" when they see their waiter with his hands full?

Doesn't it piss you off when someone asks their waiter if the "Please wash your hands" sign in the washroom is only for restaurant employees?

Doesn't it piss you off when someone asks their waiter if it's their first day, because they really suck?

Doesn't it piss you off when someone sneezes on a menu and passes it back to their waiter?

Doesn't it piss you off when someone tells their waiter to serve their meal on separate saucers?

Doesn't it piss you off when someone makes a bogus complaint to the restaurant manager about their waiter's service?

Doesn't it piss you off when someone stares at their menu for ten minutes and ignores their waiter?

Doesn't it piss you off when someone wipes their hands on their waiter's apron?

Doesn't it piss you off when someone makes a restaurant reservation and only orders breadsticks and water?

Doesn't it piss you off when someone tells the other customers coming in that the restaurant is closed?

Doesn't it piss you off when someone seats themselves in a reserved section of the restaurant and refuses to leave?

Doesn't it piss you off when someone picks up lint from the carpet and gives it to their waiter?

Doesn't it piss you off when someone puts used bubble gum on the bottom of the sugar canister?

Doesn't it piss you off when someone announces that they have allergies after their food arrives?

Doesn't it piss you off when someone sneezes and mutters "minimum wage" when their waiter's in earshot?

Doesn't it piss you off when someone picks their teeth with a toothpick and puts the toothpick back in the dispenser?

Doesn't it piss you off when a teenager tries to order from the senior's menu?

Doesn't it piss you off when someone asks their waiter for a business card?

Doesn't it piss you off when someone raises their empty glass in the air and screams out, "Refill, please!"

Doesn't it piss you off when someone requests another waiter halfway through their meal?

Doesn't it piss you off when someone blatantly tells their waiter that their dinner tasted like shit?

Doesn't it piss you off when someone screams for toilet paper from the restaurant washroom?

Doesn't it piss you off when someone says "Holy Shit!" while reviewing their bill?

Doesn't it piss you off when someone orders a seven-course meal five minutes before the restaurant closes?

Doesn't it piss you off when someone steals the fortunes out of other patrons' fortune cookies?

Doesn't it piss you off when someone yells, "Whoo!" as they open the washroom door?

Doesn't it piss you off when someone pays for their dinner with foreign currency?

Doesn't it piss you off when someone leaves a car wash token for a tip?

Doesn't it piss you off when someone smuggles an animal into the restaurant?

Doesn't it piss you off when someone repeats everything their waiter says verbatim?

Doesn't it piss you off when someone says "A.S.A.P." each time they ask for something?

Doesn't it piss you off when someone calls their waiter "Jeeves?"

Doesn't it piss you off when someone brings a picnic basket to the restaurant and only orders beverages?

Doesn't it piss you off when someone times their waiter with a stopwatch?

Doesn't it piss you off when someone makes their waiter read the entire menu to them?

Doesn't it piss you off when someone insists on eating their dinner or lunch in the shitter?

Doesn't it piss you off when someone leaves their waiter an awesome tip, but gives them a crappy survey card review?

5 GET OUT!

Doesn't it piss you off when someone asks random strangers for their autograph?

Doesn't it piss you off when someone throws car wash tokens into a wishing well?

Doesn't it piss you off when someone wears the same outfit for a month?

Doesn't it piss you off when someone throws a bunch of food into your shopping cart?

Doesn't it piss you off when someone goes jogging with handcuffs on?

Doesn't it piss you off when someone asks a prostitute if she will accept food stamps for her services?

Doesn't it piss you off when someone goes to the washroom with the door wide open?

Doesn't it piss you off when someone apologizes to the mailman for examining his package?

Doesn't it piss you off when someone listens to a salesperson give their presentation and claps when they finish?

Doesn't it piss you off when someone dresses up as Santa Claus for Halloween?

Doesn't it piss you off when someone gives a panhandler expired coupons?

Doesn't it piss you off when someone asks a shoe shiner if they have a foot fetish?

Doesn't it piss you off when someone walks into a submarine sandwich shop and asks the male sandwich artist, "Hey, is that a foot-long, or are you just happy to see me?"

Doesn't it piss you off when someone phones up 7-11 and makes reservations?

Doesn't it piss you off when someone takes a bite out of your food and runs like a bitch?

Doesn't it piss you off when someone offers their popcorn to the entire row at the movie theatre?

Doesn't it piss you off when someone files a robbery complaint with the police and then gives a description of your nation's president to the police sketch artist?

Doesn't it piss you off when you're sitting on the ground wearing a suit and someone confuses you for a panhandler and gives you a quarter?

Doesn't it piss you off when someone asks a hooker what they do for a living?

Doesn't it piss you off when someone asks identical twins how long they have known each other for?

Doesn't it piss you off when you buy someone a drink and they ask you if you used your stimulus check to pay for it?

Doesn't it piss you off when you witness someone chasing the paper boy and throwing their paper at him?

Doesn't it piss you off when someone blows their nose and examines their Kleenex?

Doesn't it piss you off when someone opens up a lemonade stand next to a pop machine?

Doesn't it piss you off when someone catches you taking a shit in a public swimming pool?

Doesn't it piss you off when someone phones the Operator and asks them what their gender is?

Doesn't it piss you off when someone messes up a department store salesman's presentation by taking a nap on the bed that they're pitching?

Doesn't it piss you off when someone goes to a busy mall food court and walks backwards?

Doesn't it piss you off when someone pushes a bunch of buttons in the elevator?

Doesn't it piss you off when someone asks you if you can see their aura?

Doesn't it piss you off when someone cheers for you every time you drop a log in a public washroom?

Doesn't it piss you off when someone sits in the silent section of the library and gets into a violent argument with themselves?

Doesn't it piss you off when someone is continuously changing seats while sitting on a public bus?

Doesn't it piss you off when someone has a long conversation on speaker while travelling on the subway?

Doesn't it piss you off when someone reads your newspaper over your shoulders?

Doesn't it piss you off when someone dines out at a ritzy restaurant wearing a straitjacket?

Doesn't it piss you off when someone picks up their children from daycare wearing a prison inmate's uniform?

Doesn't it piss you off when an unexpected relative shows up to your place and asks if you're looking for company?

Doesn't it piss you off when someone asks a senior citizen if they have an autographed copy of the Bible?

Doesn't it piss you off when someone sits in a public washroom and reads the newspaper out loud?

Doesn't it piss you off when someone walks into a conference wearing a blank name tag?

Doesn't it piss you off when someone takes a shit on the craps table at the casino?

Doesn't it piss you off when someone phones Homeland Security and asks them if the "War On Terror" is the banning of horror movies?

Doesn't it piss you off when someone drives by a teacher's strike and yells out, "Get your lazy, deadbeat asses back to work!" to the picketers?

Doesn't it piss you off when someone blatantly accuses a race car driver of being a racist?

Doesn't it piss you off when someone calls all the campers at a campground "trailer trash?"

Doesn't it piss you off when someone asks a nudist what color their underwear is?

Doesn't it piss you off when someone walks around town with a cape on?

Doesn't it piss you off when some local waits for a tourist bus to pull up and asks a tourist for directions?

Doesn't it piss you off when someone puts a leash on a stuffed animal and takes it for a walk?

Doesn't it piss you off when someone stands at the bus stop and refuses to get on the bus each time it arrives?

Doesn't it piss you off when the guy at the urinal beside you pees on your shoes?

Doesn't it piss you off when someone asks you if you washed your hands when you come out of the washroom?

Doesn't it piss you off when someone puts Weight Watchers flyers in a pregnant lady's mailbox?

Doesn't it piss you off when you ask someone for the time and they give you a hug and walk away?

Doesn't it piss you off when someone phones up a daycare and asks the receptionist if she is legally allowed to work around children?

Doesn't it piss you off when someone tells the cinema manager that there are minors hiding in the theatre and to ID everyone?

Doesn't it piss you off when someone closes the door when they see you running for the elevator?

Doesn't it piss you off when someone points and laughs at the people coming out of the beauty salon?

Doesn't it piss you off when the person sitting next to you at the movie theatre asks how much you paid to get in?

Doesn't it piss you off when someone follows you around and gives your description into their cell phone?

Doesn't it piss you off when someone phones the United Nations and asks for the KKK's phone number?

Doesn't it piss you off when your house guests are moaners?

Doesn't it piss you off when someone rings your doorbell at 3:00 AM and says, "Trick or treat?"

Doesn't it piss you off when someone asks a foreigner if they can check their Green Card?

Doesn't it piss you off when someone grabs a free sample at the grocery store, puts it behind their bum, farts on it, and then places it back on the tray?

Doesn't it piss you off when someone yells out, "YMCA!" as the flight attendant gives their emergency procedures presentation?

Doesn't it piss you off when someone makes you pick up your dog's shit at the park?

Doesn't it piss you off when someone sneezes on a buffet and then orders from the menu?

Doesn't it piss you off when a hooker asks someone if they're looking for a company and the person answers, "No, because my place is a mess?"

Doesn't it piss you off when someone repeatedly calls their pharmacist a drug dealer?

Doesn't it piss you off when someone says "ah!" after each sip of coffee?

Doesn't it piss you off when someone at the library licks their finger each time they turn a book's page?

Doesn't it piss you off when someone rips out the pages of your phone book?

Doesn't it piss you off when someone highlights every line in a newspaper while sitting in a crowded airport?

Doesn't it piss you off when someone wearing a dirty bandage on their finger continuously sticks their finger in your face?

Doesn't it piss you off when someone approaches random strangers to sign their yearbook?

Doesn't it piss you off when someone asks you for a lick of your ice cream?

Doesn't it piss you off when someone throws an unplugged toaster in a crowded swimming pool?

Doesn't it piss you off when someone drives over a muddy puddle and splashes everyone standing at the bus stop?

Doesn't it piss you off when someone observes you hailing a taxicab and steals the cab when it arrives?

Doesn't it piss you off when someone gets close to a restaurant patio and blows a dog whistle?

Doesn't it piss you off when someone orders a pizza and demands a round pizza box?

Doesn't it piss you off when someone who weighs over 400 pounds undresses with their curtains open?

Doesn't it piss you off when someone wears flip-flops in the middle of winter?

Doesn't it piss you off when someone writes a long email with their CAPS LOCK on?

Doesn't it piss you off when someone puts a Nazi scarecrow on their front lawn?

Doesn't it piss you off when someone yells "Get out!" every time somebody leaves the coffee house?

Doesn't it piss you off when a panhandler wears an expensive tuxedo while asking for money?

Doesn't it piss you off when someone R.S.V.P.s to an event and adds the disclaimer, "subject to my mood?"

Doesn't it piss you off when the person in front of you at the bank machine uses four different debit cards?

6 DUMBASS

Doesn't it piss you off when a hooker refuses to give you a senior discount?

Doesn't it piss you off when someone wears two different-colored socks?

Doesn't it piss you off when a four-hundred-pound male plumber with baggy pants wears thong underwear?

Doesn't it piss you off when someone wears a helmet on the bus?

Doesn't it piss you off when a hooker doesn't offer frequent flyer miles?

Doesn't it piss you off when the venereal disease clinic doesn't offer frequent flyer miles?

Doesn't it piss you off when someone pulls off their dirty bandage and asks you if their finger is healed?

Doesn't it piss you off when someone purposely chews loudly during the silent parts of a movie?

Doesn't it piss you off when the person in front of you at the bank wants to deposit one hundred dollars in unrolled pennies?

Doesn't it piss you off when someone keeps making a toast each time they have a drink?

Doesn't it piss you off when someone makes grunting sounds when working out at the gym?

Doesn't it piss you off when someone asks a hooker if they are a virgin?

Doesn't it piss you off when your neighbor knocks on your door at 3:00 AM to borrow some sugar?

Doesn't it piss you off when someone finishes their cereal and pours the milk back in the carton?

Doesn't it piss you off when someone wears a tuxedo or an evening gown to McDonald's?

Doesn't it piss you off when someone tells you that you missed a spot when you're mopping the floor?

Doesn't it piss you off when someone wears ripped jeans and a tank top to a ritzy restaurant?

Doesn't it piss you off when someone tells you to turn on the washroom fan after you take a dump?

Doesn't it piss you off when someone continuously yawns during a movie?

Doesn't it piss you off when a hooker refuses to give you a receipt?

Doesn't it piss you off when the accused person on trial refuses to swear on the Bible?

Doesn't it piss you off when someone who is wearing a watch asks you what time it is?

Doesn't it piss you off when someone who is eight months pregnant wears a belly top?

Doesn't it piss you off when someone stands outside the gym window eating a foot-long submarine sandwich?

Doesn't it piss you off when a hooker refuses to give you a payment plan?

Doesn't it piss you off when someone sticks their head in the sewer and asks the city workers if they have any toilet paper down there?

Doesn't it piss you off when someone makes the grocery store bagger carry a loaf of bread to their car?

Doesn't it piss you off when someone requests a security escort to walk them to their car after they win $10 at the casino?

Doesn't it piss you off when someone asks a hooker what they want to be when they grow up?

Doesn't it piss you off when you get kicked out of sex education class for asking too many questions?

Doesn't it piss you off when someone goes to confession and tells the priest that they are cheating on their diet?

Doesn't it piss you off when someone yells out, "I'm just browsing," as they walk into a department store?

Doesn't it piss you off when someone cuts their toenails in the produce department of the grocery store?

Doesn't it piss you off when a hooker refuses to say whether they are religious?

Doesn't it piss you off when someone who is fluent in English enrolls in ESL class?

Doesn't it piss you off when someone drives a convertible car with the top down in the middle of winter?

Doesn't it piss you off when someone refuses to take their shoes off at a Japanese restaurant?

Doesn't it piss you off when someone calls the helpline and asks for directions on how to cook Kraft dinner?

Doesn't it piss you off when someone asks their banker for a free sample?

Doesn't it piss you off when someone uses your finger to pick their nose?

Doesn't it piss you off when someone pees on your back as you're standing in line for the washroom?

Doesn't it piss you off when a hooker refuses to give you directions to a brothel?

Doesn't it piss you off when a pimp doesn't offer a retirement plan to his staff?

Doesn't it piss you off when a hooker doesn't stand behind her product?

Doesn't it piss you off when someone uses the corner of the counter to scratch their ass?

Doesn't it piss you off when someone squirts a store perfume tester on their ass?

Doesn't it piss you off when someone uses your toothbrush to clean their toilets?

Doesn't it piss you off when someone dribbles a basketball everywhere they go?

Doesn't it piss you off when someone throws their bowling ball down your alley?

Doesn't it piss you off when someone teaches their parrot to swear at you?

Doesn't it piss you off when someone uses your computer and bookmarks porn websites?

Doesn't it piss you off when someone borrows your underwear without your permission and then returns it with a thank-you card?

Doesn't it piss you off when someone borrows your car and leaves love stains on your back seat?

Doesn't it piss you off when someone reads over your shoulder and shouts out the answers to your trivia question cards?

Doesn't it piss you off when a Monopoly player writes a letter to Congress and requests a bailout loan?

Doesn't it piss you off when someone lets out the raunchiest fart at the blackjack table?

Doesn't it piss you off when someone asks a garage sale host if they are selling something new?

Doesn't it piss you off when someone asks the airline for a bereavement fare for their honeymoon?
Doesn't it piss you off when someone attempts to shop for brand new antiques?

Doesn't it piss you off when someone serves airline food at a dinner party?

Doesn't it piss you off when someone tells you to bring your own toilet paper to their party?

Doesn't it piss you off when someone takes a shit in your washroom sink?

Doesn't it piss you off when someone charges their friends to use their toilet?

Doesn't it piss you off when someone walks around with a shower cap?

Doesn't it piss you off when someone tries to sell you a free sample?

Doesn't it piss you off when someone phones MasterCard and asks questions about the weather?

Doesn't it piss you off when someone rides a bicycle to a biker bar?

Doesn't it piss you off when someone charges you double for last week's newspaper?

Doesn't it piss you off when someone walks around the mall wearing a life preserver?

Doesn't it piss you off when someone asks a hooker for their credentials?

Doesn't it piss you off when someone leaves a used tampon in your mailbox?

Doesn't it piss you off when your boyfriend tells you that your grandmother is hot?

Doesn't it piss you off when your boyfriend negotiates the price of your anniversary gift at the dollar store?

Doesn't it piss you off when a telemarketer promises to take you off their list and then gives you a wake-up call the next morning?

Doesn't it piss you off when a hooker refuses to accept your Groupon?

7 NEIGHBORS

Doesn't it piss you off when your neighbor takes your Christmas lights and hangs them on their house?

Doesn't it piss you off when your neighbor bakes you some homemade laxative brownies?

Doesn't it piss you off when your neighbor Saran Wraps your doorway?

Doesn't it piss you off when your neighbor rubs poop all over your car and house door handles?

Doesn't it piss you off when your neighbor passes around after-hours party flyers at the bar with your address on it?

Doesn't it piss you off when your neighbor orders you a mail-order bride?

Doesn't it piss you off when your neighbor gets your car towed?

Doesn't it piss you off when your neighbor puts a bunch of pornographic DVDs on your porch?

Doesn't it piss you off when your neighbor puts an ad on Craigslist for a garage sale at your place without telling you?

Doesn't it piss you off when your neighbor puts a burning bag of dog doo-doo on your porch, rings your doorbell, and then runs like a bitch?

Doesn't it piss you off when your neighbor dumps a box of nails on your driveway?

Doesn't it piss you off when your neighbor hangs their soiled underwear on your clothing line?

Doesn't it piss you off when your neighbor fills your voicemail with vocals from a pornographic movie?

Doesn't it piss you off when your neighbor draws a chalk sketch of a dead body on your driveway?

Doesn't it piss you off when your neighbor toilet-papers your house?

Doesn't it piss you off when your neighbor throws unwrapped bite-sized chocolate bars in your swimming pool?

Doesn't it piss you off when your neighbor dumps a wheelbarrow full of used tampons on your sundeck?

Doesn't it piss you off when your neighbor plugs an extension cord in your outlet and uses your power to mow their lawn?

Doesn't it piss you off when your neighbor throws their shit in your garbage can?

Doesn't it piss you off when your neighbor pisses on your barbecue grill?

Doesn't it piss you off when your neighbor takes little bites of the fruit on your trees?

Doesn't it piss you off when neighbor steals food off your barbecue?

Doesn't it piss you off when your neighbor lets their dog loose in your backyard?

Doesn't it piss you off when your neighbor puts a tombstone on your lawn?

Doesn't it piss you off when your neighbor turns your hose on when you're not looking?

Doesn't it piss you off when your neighbor takes a shit in your air conditioner vents?

Doesn't it piss you off when your neighbor complains to the authorities that you're beating your pet?

Doesn't it piss you off when your neighbor hires a locksmith to change your locks?

Doesn't it piss you off when your neighbor puts a "For Sale By Owner" sign on your lawn?

Doesn't it piss you off when your neighbor tries to confuse you by pouring antifreeze under your car?

Doesn't it piss you off when your neighbor calls the utility company and gets your gas and electricity shut off?

Doesn't it piss you off when your neighbor puts a phony eviction notice on your door?

Doesn't it piss you off when your neighbor puts condoms on the end of your garden hose?

Doesn't it piss you off when your neighbor arranges twenty different taxicabs to come to your house at 2:30 AM?

Doesn't it piss you off when your neighbor picks the flowers out of your garden and sends you a bouquet?

Doesn't it piss you off when your neighbor has sex on your lawn furniture?

Doesn't it piss you off when you're in your swimming pool and your neighbor turns their sprinkler on?

Doesn't it piss you off when your neighbor sends a transsexual hooker to your house?

Doesn't it piss you off when your neighbor urinates in your iced tea when you're not looking?

Doesn't it piss you off when your neighbor refers their door-to-door salesmen to you and claims that you're their landlord?

Doesn't it piss you off when your neighbor orders you a C.O.D. bouquet of flowers?

Doesn't it piss you off when your neighbor pours laundry detergent in your swimming pool?

Doesn't it piss you off when your neighbor writes your new phone number on the bathroom wall of a greasy biker bar?

Doesn't it piss you off when your neighbor talks to people on various transvestite dating websites and gives your phone number out?

Doesn't it piss you off when your neighbor schedules you a 4:00 AM wakeup call?

Doesn't it piss you off when your neighbor puts a "Just Married" sign on the back of your car along with some streamers and pop cans?

Doesn't it piss you off when your neighbor parks in your driveway?

Doesn't it piss you off when your neighbor randomly sets off your car alarm in the middle of the night?

Doesn't it piss you off when neighbor puts a condom on your muffler?

Doesn't it piss you off when your neighbor puts fake parking tickets on your windshield?

Doesn't it piss you off when your neighbor secretly takes pictures of you and places the pictures on your car windshield?

Doesn't it piss you off when your neighbor waits until you have finished washing your car before giving a pressure wash to their dirty driveway?

Doesn't it piss you off when your neighbor puts a "I Love Nazis" bumper sticker on your fender?

Doesn't it piss you off when your neighbor puts a CPR dummy with ketchup all over it under your car?

Doesn't it piss you off when your neighbor takes off in your car, which you were trying to warm up?

Doesn't it piss you off when your neighbor opens your mail and tells everyone on the block that you're about to lose your house?

Doesn't it piss you off when your neighbor takes a piss in your mail slot?

Doesn't it piss you off when your neighbor gets a universal TV remote control and changes your channels for you?

Doesn't it piss you off when your four-hundred-pound neighbors have sex with their curtains open?

Doesn't it piss you off when your neighbor puts your name and number on restaurant survey cards?

Doesn't it piss you off when your neighbor rubs a baseball in dog pooh and throws it at you?

Doesn't it piss you off when your neighbor shines a flashlight through your bathroom window when you're taking a dump?

Doesn't it piss you off when your neighbor plays peek-a-boo through their window every time you go outside?

Doesn't it piss you off when your neighbor removes the "This house is protected by XYZ Alarm Company" stickers from your windows and doors?

Doesn't it piss you off when your neighbor's kids crash a remote-control plane through your window?

Doesn't it piss you off when your neighbor paints your windows black?

Doesn't it piss you off when you catch your neighbor in bed with your wife?

Doesn't it piss you off when your neighbor does a change-of-address on your behalf to a location on the other side of the planet?

Doesn't it piss you off when your neighbor rearranges your outside address digits?

Doesn't it piss you off when your neighbor cooks stinky chicken curry when your windows are open?

Doesn't it piss you off when your neighbor steals sections of your newspaper?

Doesn't it piss you off when your neighbor recycles their used condoms in your mailbox?

Doesn't it piss you off when your neighbor fills your name and address on one hundred different catalogue request forms?

Doesn't it piss you off when your neighbor pours bleach on your lawn?

Doesn't it piss you off when your neighbor sends anonymous love letters to your grandmother?

Doesn't it piss you off when your neighbor steals your porch lightbulbs?

Doesn't it piss you off when your neighbor punctures your basketball?

Doesn't it piss you off when your neighbor glues a couple of quarters on your driveway?

8 COWORKERS

Doesn't it piss you off when your coworker leaves a present for you in the toilet?

Doesn't it piss you off when your coworker leaves their dirty dishes in the sink?

Doesn't it piss you off when your coworker brings ice to a potluck dinner?

Doesn't it piss you off when your coworker steals food out of your lunch bag and writes "Ha Ha!" on it?

Doesn't it piss you off when your coworker microwaves stinky curry?

Doesn't it piss you off when your coworker counts out loud?

Doesn't it piss you off when your coworker who sits next to you emails you with a request to lower your voice?

Doesn't it piss you off when your coworker wears the exact same outfit that you're wearing?

Doesn't it piss you off when your coworker borrows money off you and quits their job before paying you back?

Doesn't it piss you off when your coworker gets their friends to make bogus customer service complaints about you?

Doesn't it piss you off when your coworker goes to the washroom with the door open?

Doesn't it piss you off when your coworker hides all the toilet paper in the washroom ceiling?

Doesn't it piss you off when your coworker circles classified ads and leaves them on your desk?

Doesn't it piss you off when your coworker tells you a rumor that your company is going bankrupt?

Doesn't it piss you off when your coworker deposits your paycheck into their account?

Doesn't it piss you off when your coworker hits on your significant other at the company Christmas party?

Doesn't it piss you off when your coworker questions you about everything on your Facebook wall?

Doesn't it piss you off when your coworker gives your home number to all of your clients?

Doesn't it piss you off when your coworker resets your computer each time you go to the shitter?

Doesn't it piss you off when your coworker scratches their crotch and winks at you?

Doesn't it piss you off when your coworker invites everyone except you to the pub after work?

Doesn't it piss you off when your coworker shows you a phony paystub, claiming they earn more than you?

Doesn't it piss you off when your coworker orders you a strip-o-gram at work?

Doesn't it piss you off when your coworker doesn't pay their share of tax and tip after a group meal?

Doesn't it piss you off when your coworker tells angry customers that you are the manager when you aren't?

Doesn't it piss you off when your coworker constantly volunteers you?

Doesn't it piss you off when your coworker puts tape on the bottom of your mouse?

Doesn't it piss you off when your coworker addresses you by your title and not your name?

Doesn't it piss you off when your coworker forwards you their junk mail?

Doesn't it piss you off when your coworker takes a twenty-minute shit break?

Doesn't it piss you off when your coworker uses a competitor's products at work?

Doesn't it piss you off when your coworker sends you one-word emails?

Doesn't it piss you off when your coworker clocks you out early?

Doesn't it piss you off when your coworker doesn't carry their weight?

Doesn't it piss you off when your coworker pawns their shit off on you?

Doesn't it piss you off when your coworker sends you text messages from the washroom?

Doesn't it piss you off when your coworker tells your colleagues that you were at the abortion clinic on your day off?

Doesn't it piss you off when your coworker accuses you of going on a job interview the day you called in sick?

Doesn't it piss you off when your coworker high-fives you after coming out of the washroom?

Doesn't it piss you off when your coworker gets everyone to leave the breakroom as you walk in?

Doesn't it piss you off when your coworker photocopies their bare ass and emails it to you?

Doesn't it piss you off when your coworker sings along with the radio?

Doesn't it piss you off when your coworker chews their food loudly?

Doesn't it piss you off when your coworker, who's sitting beside you, pages you on the intercom?

Doesn't it piss you off when your coworker pokes their head in the boardroom when your boss is giving you shit?

Doesn't it piss you off when your coworker puts caffeinated coffee in the decaf coffee jug?

Doesn't it piss you off when your coworker announces exactly how long you were in the washroom when you come out?

Doesn't it piss you off when your coworker hangs up the phone on you without saying goodbye?

Doesn't it piss you off when your coworker walks around the office barefoot?

Doesn't it piss you off when your coworker uses their picture as your screen saver?

9 ROOMMATES

Doesn't it piss you off when your roommate spits on the taps and doesn't wipe it off?

Doesn't it piss you off when your roommate urinates in your mouthwash?

Doesn't it piss you off when your roommate sleeps with your girlfriend?

Doesn't it piss you off when your roommate makes you write down where you're going and when you're coming back?

Doesn't it piss you off when your roommate transfers a telemarketing call to you?

Doesn't it piss you off when your roommate doesn't pay their share of the rent and tells your landlord that you're a deadbeat?

Doesn't it piss you off when your roommate allows their dog to sleep in your bed?

Doesn't it piss you off when your roommate has sex in your bed?

Doesn't it piss you off when your roommate takes a bite out of your food?

Doesn't it piss you off when your roommate borrows your underwear?

Doesn't it piss you off when your roommate gives themselves a pedicure with your butter knife?

Doesn't it piss you off when your roommate watches you sleep?

Doesn't it piss you off when your roommate sleepwalks nude?

Doesn't it piss you off when your roommate takes pictures of you sleeping?

Doesn't it piss you off when your roommate hides portable alarm clocks underneath your bed?

Doesn't it piss you off when your roommate pisses in your plants?

Doesn't it piss you off when your roommate deletes your voicemail messages?

Doesn't it piss you off when your roommate puts up a "roommate wanted" newspaper ad?

Doesn't it piss you off when your roommate donates all your shit to charity?

Doesn't it piss you off when your roommate moves into your parents' house?

Doesn't it piss you off when your roommate turns off the water when you're in the shower?

Doesn't it piss you off when your roommate double-dips their chips?

Doesn't it piss you off when your roommate sits right next you when you're watching TV?

Doesn't it piss you off when your roommate twists their nipples and winks at you when you're talking to your landlord?

Doesn't it piss you off when your roommate puts a "Please wash your hands" sign in your washroom?

Doesn't it piss you off when your roommate unplugs your alarm clock?

Doesn't it piss you off when your roommate tells your welfare officer that you are working for cash?

Doesn't it piss you off when your roommate follows you around the apartment like a shadow?

Doesn't it piss you off when your roommate divides the apartment in half?

Doesn't it piss you off when your roommate accuses you of hitting on their imaginary boyfriend?

Doesn't it piss you off when your roommate uses chopsticks to eat everything?

Doesn't it piss you off when your roommate cooks fish in the microwave?

Doesn't it piss you off when your roommate tells your boss where you really were on your sick day?

Doesn't it piss you off when your roommate gives their friends copies of your apartment key?

Doesn't it piss you off when your roommate licks you while you're asleep?

Doesn't it piss you off when your roommate panhandles in front of your apartment?

Doesn't it piss you off when your roommate schedules an intervention for you?

Doesn't it piss you off when your roommate takes notes each time you speak?

Doesn't it piss you off when your roommate moves your bed into the hallway?

Doesn't it piss you off when your roommate puts the TV remote control in their underwear?

Doesn't it piss you off when your roommate puts a ski mask, rope, and knife in your closet?

Doesn't it piss you off when your roommate requests that you give them a massage with a happy ending?

Doesn't it piss you off when your roommate puts earplugs on when you're talking?

Doesn't it piss you off when your roommate reads your diary and highlights your fuck-ups?

Doesn't it piss you off when your roommate opens all your windows while you're sleeping?

Doesn't it piss you off when your roommate hangs a CPR dummy off your balcony?

Doesn't it piss you off when your roommate joins you in the shower?

Doesn't it piss you off when your roommate walks by your bedroom naked and waves at you?

Doesn't it piss you off when your roommate watches porn with the volume blaring?

Doesn't it piss you off when your roommate shreds documents at 4:00 AM?

Doesn't it piss you off when your roommate lends your shit to their friends?

Doesn't it piss you off when your roommate opens a doggy-daycare in your bedroom?

Doesn't it piss you off when your roommate constantly changes the TV channels?

Doesn't it piss you off when your roommate puts naked pictures of you in the cereal box?

Doesn't it piss you off when your roommate moves out when you're on vacation?

Doesn't it piss you off when your roommate stares at the TV for hours while it's turned off?

Doesn't it piss you off when your roommate tells you about your surprise birthday party?

Doesn't it piss you off when your roommate slips notes underneath the washroom door when you're taking a shit?

Doesn't it piss you off when your roommate uses your shaver to shave their private parts?

10 CRAPPY STUDENTS

Doesn't it piss you off when your student puts a half-eaten apple on your desk?

Doesn't it piss you off when your student asks you for assistance during an exam?

Doesn't it piss you off when your student asks you what you really wanted to do for a profession?

Doesn't it piss you off when your student asks you if you're legally allowed to work with minors?

Doesn't it piss you off when your student constantly asks you what time it is?

Doesn't it piss you off when your student panhandles in front of the classroom for school supplies?

Doesn't it piss you off when a student yells out "dumbass" each time their peers say the wrong answer?

Doesn't it piss you off when your student volunteers to solve a problem on the blackboard when they have a woody?

Doesn't it piss you off when your students yell out "deadbeat" while you're on strike?

Doesn't it piss you off when your student constantly winks at you?

Doesn't it piss you off when your student completes an entire exam in crayon?

Doesn't it piss you off when your student whispers their responses?

Doesn't it piss you off when your student asks you when the last time you showered was?

Doesn't it piss you off when your student gives you a deodorant stick for Christmas?

Doesn't it piss you off when your students complain to the principal that they aren't learning anything?

Doesn't it piss you off when your student asks you if this is your first year teaching?

Doesn't it piss you off when your student keeps calling you "hon?"

Doesn't it piss you off when your student asks you for proof that you graduated from high school?

Doesn't it piss you off when your students laugh at you when you're on strike?

Doesn't it piss you off when your student gives you a "Teaching For Dummies" book?

Doesn't it piss you off when your student gets pizza delivered to class?

Doesn't it piss you off when your student asks you to autograph their textbook?

Doesn't it piss you off when your students ask questions in knock-knock joke format?

Doesn't it piss you off when you bust your students passing around blank notes?

Doesn't it piss you off when your students staple their homework in the middle of the page?

Doesn't it piss you off when your student screams out, "Oww, I'm sorry," each time the principal walks by?

Doesn't it piss you off when your student hands you a bag of dog shit as proof that their dog ate their homework?

Doesn't it piss you off when your student waves at everyone that passes by in the hallway?

Doesn't it piss you off when your student tells you that they finished their homework on the toilet after passing it to you?

Doesn't it piss you off when your students call you by your first name?

Doesn't it piss you off when your student yawns out loud while you're lecturing?

Doesn't it piss you off when your student follows you around spraying perfume on your butt?

Doesn't it piss you off when your student does his homework on restaurant napkins?

Doesn't it piss you off when your students constantly ask you if you can back up what you're teaching?

Doesn't it piss you off when your student replaces historical figures with names of your school's teaching faculty?

Doesn't it piss you off when your student asks you how much money you make?

Doesn't it piss you off when your student asks you for an extension as soon as you assign something?

Doesn't it piss you off when your student shows up to class an hour late and leaves class fifteen minutes early?

Doesn't it piss you off when your student yells out "Bingo!" each time you ask a question?

Doesn't it piss you off when your student eats laxatives and keeps running to the shitter?

Doesn't it piss you off when your student has a mannequin arm sticking out of their bag?

Doesn't it piss you off when your students tell you that they prefer their substitute teacher to you?

Doesn't it piss you off when your student skips your class and leaves a CPR dummy sitting in their spot?

Doesn't it piss you off when your student moves their head away from you when you're speaking, pretending you have breath?

Doesn't it piss you off when your student attempts to bribe you with Fruit Roll-Ups to change their grades?

Doesn't it piss you off when your student refuses to remove the shrink-wrap from their textbook?

Doesn't it piss you off when your student asks you a question that requires a long-ass answer and then silently farts as you explain?

ABOUT THE AUTHOR

Sidney S. Prasad is an author on a quest to make the world laugh. His work is focused on entertaining people with his dry-humored novels. Sidney S. Prasad personally believes laughter is the best cure for all of life's ups and downs.

Some other humorous books written by Sidney S. Prasad include:

How To Piss Off A Telemarketer,
How To Piss Off A Salesman
My Bipolar Manager,
Don't Ask Dumb Questions!,
Corny Names & Stupid Places,
Misfortune Cookies,
My Stupid CEO,
Plenty Of Freaks: Are You Sold On Online Dating?
Plenty Of Freaks: Worst Online Dating Mistakes
Plenty Of Freaks: Is Dating Legalized Prostitution?
and
Telemarketer's Revenge: The Customer Is Always Wrong, Bitch!